# Good Dog!

by Susan Ring

Consultant: Robyn Barbiers, General Curator,
Lincoln Park Zoo, Chicago, Illinois

Yellow Umbrella Books are published by Red Brick Learning
7825 Telegraph Road, Bloomington, Minnesota 55438
http://www.redbricklearning.com

Editorial Director: Mary Lindeen
Senior Editor: Hollie J. Endres
Senior Designer: Gene Bentdahl
Photo Researcher: Signature Design
Developer: Raindrop Publishing
Consultant: Robyn Barbiers, General Curator, Lincoln Park Zoo, Chicago, Illinois
Conversion Assistants: Jenny Marks, Laura Manthe

*Library of Congress Cataloging-in-Publication Data*
Ring, Susan
Good Dog! / by Susan Ring
p. cm.
ISBN 0-7368-5839-3 (hardcover)
ISBN 0-7368-5269-7 (softcover)
1. Dogs—Juvenile literature. I. Title. II. Series.
SF426.5.R58 2005
636.7—dc22

2005016209


Printed in the United States of America

Photo Credits:
Cover: Image Source Photos; Title Page: Brand X Pictures; Page 2: Corbis; Page 3: Tom Nebbia/Corbis; Pages 4 and 5: PhotoDisc Images; Page 6: AP/Wide World Photos; Page 7: Bob Crisp; The Daily Home/AP/Wide World Photos; Page 8: Tom Carroll/ZUMA Press; Page 9: Nina Long; The Tennessean/AP/Wide World Photos; Page 10: Sangjib Min; The Daily Press/AP/Wide World Photos; Page 11: Corbis; Page 12: The Kennel Club Picture Library; Page 13: Guzelian Photography; Page 14: Corel; Page 15: Greg Lynch; Journal News/AP/Wide World Photos

1 2 3 4 5 6 11 10 09 08 07 06

# Table of Contents

# Introduction

Dogs make great pets. They play ball. They run and jump. They **guard** the house. Dogs are good company.

Dogs also help people. Many dogs have important jobs to do. Some even go to school to learn their jobs.

# On the Go

These sheep roam free and eat grass. The farmer doesn't want any sheep to get lost. How does he keep them together?

He gets help from his **herding dog**. The dog barks and runs. He keeps the sheep in one place. Good dog!

This blind person gets help from her **guide dog**. She holds on to his **harness**. He guides her as they walk. She takes him everywhere.

The dog uses his eyes and ears. He makes sure that it's safe to cross the street. He knows what to do. Good dog!

# Training

Guide dogs are gentle and smart. When they are puppies, they learn simple things. They learn how to sit and stay.

When they are older, they go to a special school. People **train** them to be guide dogs. After a few months, the dogs are matched with owners.

# Super Senses

This dog works with the police. He helps find people who are missing. He uses his nose to pick up a **scent**. Good dog!

Could you find a person under all this snow? This dog can. She also uses her **sense** of smell. She will bark to say that she found someone. Good dog!

# Around the House

Even a little dog can be a big help. This dog helps a person who can't hear. The dog knows what to listen for. He lets his owner know when the doorbell rings.

Dogs can also turn on lights and open doors. Some even know how to use the phone! This dog wears a special coat. It lets people know she is working.

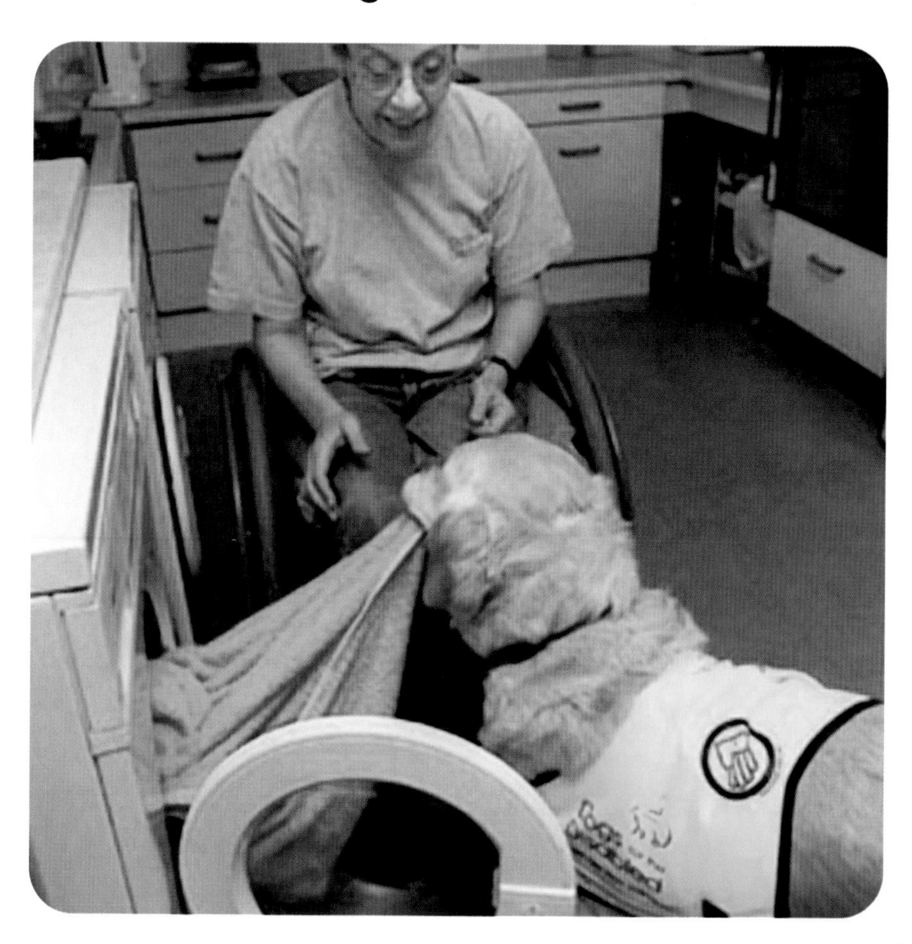

# Just for Fun

These dogs are running a long race in **Alaska**. They like to race and have fun as they work hard. They will run for hours every day in the snow.

This dog is having fun as she runs and jumps. She has a lot of energy. She is trying to win a contest, but it is okay if she doesn't. She is still a very good dog!

# Glossary

**Alaska**—largest state in the U.S.

**guard**—to protect or watch over

**guide dog**—a dog that is trained to work with blind people

**harness**—a strap attached to a dog, with a handle for a person to hold on to

**herding dog**—a dog that gathers and looks after sheep or cattle

**scent**—a smell

**sense**—the ability to see, hear, smell, touch or taste

**train**—to teach

# Index



Word Count: 363
Early-Intervention Level: J